eBay Selling For Beginners:

Ultimate guide to reselling online

By Jennifer Galegor

Table of Contents

INTRO

During a time where we don't know what our future looks like, control your own destiny.

Hello, and welcome to my book. I know, cheesy intro, but what else do you say to a bunch of strangers you've never met? While I do not expect you to jump up and down with excitement when you read this, I do hope you enjoy what I have to say and teach.

My family consists of my husband Bret and I, along with our two children. I started an online reselling business in 2019. My firstborn was about to start Kindergarten and I knew I would have time on my hands. Having been married almost 10 years, my husband and I do everything together. So, when I told him I wanted to find something to do to keep me busy, and bring a little extra money to the household, he was on board. I am a stay-at-home mom and have heard of every "Work from Home" job on the planet. None of them seemed to be a fit for me. But I have always had a love for and a background in sales, so I decided I wanted to nurture that. What started as a hobby, quickly became much more.

I had recently discovered an entrepreneur online that mentioned he did this as a side hustle. He began his video emphasizing the ease of selling online, and how cheap it could be to start out. Even buying items at a garage sale for 25¢! Sure they asked for $1, but nope, he offered a quarter. Using his videos to light that fire under my butt, I soaked in every ounce of knowledge he was giving out.

Days went buy, and I began keeping an eye out for garage sales and estate sales in my area. Multiple apps showed where some were and by driving around, I seemed to find even more. I searched thrift stores and flea markets for anything and everything I could sell online. After all, if this other guy could do it, so could I. I found my first *loot* and heard my first *cha-ching* and I was sold!

Stay put, take notes, and have fun, while I tell you all my tips and tricks for selling online and creating your own stimulus!

CHAPTER 1

As I'm sure you've noticed, I use eBay as my main platform. Sure there are others, Mercari, Etsy, Amazon, and Facebook Marketplace. I tend to keep 95% of my selling on eBay. Hey, free traffic! I do use Facebook for larger items. Things I do not want to ship. However, eBay just makes things easy, and relatively cheap, so why reinvent the wheel?

When you are first starting out on eBay, it is best to start with things you already own. Why spend money on inventory when you could clean out your closets, garage, basement, or that old toy box for *free* inventory? Gather anything you think has some value; electronics, video games, name brand clothes and shoes, old pots and pans, etc. The list goes on. I will go over a list of items to always keep an eye out for later in this book.

Gather that box of goodies and begin to research what these items are worth. Download the *eBay* app on your smartphone for a hands-on tool, right in your pocket.

While this first lesson has you gathering items you think are worth money, you will quickly learn what you *think* will sell, may not. Items that may make you think "No one would ever buy that!"… wait and be surprised!

Best thing you could do right now is get familiar with eBay, the marketplace, the website, and the app. Play around with looking stuff up and then seeing what it sold for.

Search for the item

Click "FILTER" on the top right

Scroll and select "SOLD ITEMS"

This is where you see what the item *actually* sells for. Not just what it is listed at.

Once you have looked up the item, note how many are available, and then select "SOLDS" (under filter as described above) and see how many *actually* sold. **The golden ticket is when an item has more "solds" than available.** This tells us there is more demand than what is out there. This should lead to a quick sale at the going rate. Keep in mind what the others are selling for. I like to price somewhere in the middle and always turn on Offers. "Offers" allows a buyer to make you an offer, which you can either accept or counter. This feature has worked well with me. If I feel they are low-balling me, I just counter with what I feel is fair. I always keep in mind what I actually paid for this item to make sure it's still profitable, but still giving the buyer the feeling of a good deal.

Ok, so you have found your item. You see there is more sold, or at least 50% or so, of what's available. You are ready to list your first item!

Once you are in a sold listing, you can click the "Sell Similar" option. This pulls all relevant information from the current listing, giving you a head start on yours. You will then need to fill in a few spots including pictures, price, description, and variants like color, size, etc. You will also want to double check the shipping selection. Make sure to put in the correct weight and dimensions of the box this is going into. I will go into shipping information in another chapter too so don't get too confused right now. Making sure you select "CALCULATED SHIPPING" in the options.

There you have it, your first listing.

CHAPTER 2
SOURCING

Where

As a new reseller, the best start for sourcing, as I mentioned previously, is your own house. After you have cleaned house, basement, and any other nook and cranny, it's time to hit the streets! Thrift stores are probably my favorite place to source. You get to look at stuff with no pressure, no one looking over your shoulder. You can take your time to look items up. My favorite reason is no haggling. Sure it's nice to get a good deal, but I feel at garage sales its more pressure to make sure you don't pay more than what it's worth. You have added pressure to not offend the seller by low-balling, and sometimes it's just awkward. Don't get me wrong, I *LOVE* a good garage sale! I just prefer thrift stores.

When I enter the thrift store, I usually start on one end and work my way over and around, focusing my attention on electronics and hard goods. I will go over other categories, but you will notice I favor that one for sure. A few big-name thrift stores are Goodwill, Arc, and The Salvation Army. You may be lucky to have some smaller ones in your area, but those are usually hit or miss. Pricing tends to be higher in smaller shops to cover their overhead. Always look for their "weak spot", meaning the category they don't know so well. Every thrift and estate sale cannot know every category. You will get to know some better than others. So just enter with an open mind, scan *all kinds of items,* and learn.

Estate sales are probably my next favorite source. Those run by families are the best since they just want to make money for the family, no profit in their pockets. Big name estate companies will always mark up their items. I always giggle when they either say, or post a picture of what the item sells for on eBay. Sadly, they don't go by what sold, just what that person thinks they can sell it for. Estate sale locations can also be found with a national site or app. There are a couple I use, *estatesales.org* and *estatesales.net.* They both will list sales in your area and, if they have them, pictures of what's at that sale. I like to get a sneak peek and start studying what they have so I know what I am after *before* I get there.

Estates are known for vintage items, being most estate sales are for selling items after someone has passed away. You can either start to learn vintage, or just keep an eye out for things you already know. I like to make it a goal to always look up new items I see. This holds true for all sourcing. If you don't know what it is, and it looks interesting, look it up. I have found some very interesting items by doing so. Ever heard of a water ionizer? Me neither, till I sold one. I also keep an eye out for old razors or even beauty products, new in the box, as those seem to hold value as well. Another shocker that is great to find at estate sales is new socks and underwear. You would be surprised how many people buy packs and never open them. There is a huge market for these items. Think of your favorite t-shirt, worn to just your shape, has your smell, your favorite color, neck shape just how you like it and then it gets a hole! You would do everything you could to replace that shirt. Same goes for underwear and socks. Once you like something you like to keep buying that item. Manufacturers change their product far too often, and not everyone likes that new formula. So always keep an eye out for unopened, old stock clothing.

Be prepared for *every* estate sale you go to. Try to arrive early if you can, bring cash, and a bag. These sales are usually pretty busy, and you will quickly fill your arms with items you want. I never trust a hold table. Maybe that's just me. Having a large canvas bag, such as the ones from *Ikea* or even grocery stores, comes in handy. You can always spot a fellow reseller by that lovely *Ikea* bag.

Last, but not least, are garage sales. While this isn't my favorite way to source, it's always the most consistent. You can find sales in your area using social media, or even an app called *Yard Sale Treasure Hunt*. This is a great tool to gather local sales. However, I do find those sales are quickly picked through since they were advertised. My best scores have always been the random sale with a sign at the end of the street. Garage sales are great because you can always negotiate and get really good deals. I personally find it awkward to look stuff up at the sale, but honestly everyone is on their phone these days so it's not out of the ordinary for you to be on your phone. Once you get more experience you will be able to spot items before looking them up. I will sometimes just walk around the table, do a quick search, and then go back. I am sure that's pretty obvious, but I think it looks less rude. Experience is the best education you can get in this business. While I find estate sales more fun than garage sales, you may find differently. While I love electronics and hard goods, you may like clothing or antiques. That's the beauty of this. There is always something for everyone. You will find your niche and really master it. Keeping an open mind to expand that expertise is key. Nothing like leaving money on the table because you don't know that arena.

There are other ways to source that I won't go into much detail about, and that's *Facebook Marketplace, Mercari, Offer Up, Craigslist,* and even friends and family. These are great to check out once in a while, but I don't hold out much hope for those. Sure, I have got a few good finds on Marketplace, but usually I am too late, and the item sells too fast, if it's priced where I want it. Probably because they listed it low enough for us resellers, and someone else was faster than I was. The other items are listed for eBay prices on Marketplace, so leaving no meat on the bone for us.

Pallets, liquidations, Amazon returns— again, items I don't go after. I am not looking for volume, I am looking for quality. I don't want to fill up my garage with pallets of returned cosmetics, or opened items that will take too long to sell. I would rather scope out individual items and list accordingly. That's my cup of tea.

What

I have mentioned multiple times in this book what I like to look for. What exactly do I mean when I say electronics? Why do I like electronics? Well, I am always looking for anything with a model number. I am also watching out for big names; Sony, Apple, Sonos, and more. These items keep their value. When I find an item that catches my interest, I simply search by that make and model. Electronics are great because there are no variations on that item. If it's a Sony Blu Ray Model S3700 there is only one of that model. I am not trying to match color, or shape, or anything. It's one model and that's it. Simple search and sold research. When you get into other categories it's a lot harder to find an exact comparables (comps.) Cabbage Patch Doll's for example: brown hair, yellow hair, blue dress, pink dress, 1980s, 1970s, and so on. Same for many clothes and some other categories. I like an item that's easy and quick to comp. Not to say that's the easiest category to sell.

You will find some challenges with electronics, and that's why a lot of resellers avoid them. Testing is the first one. You will *always* want to test your items. That being said, you need a way to test it. For instance, I get a lot of DVD-VCR combo players. You will need AV cables, and a TV. You will always want a VHS to play in it, and a DVD. These are items you can easily gather at thrift stores while you're sourcing. I keep a bin of

AV cables, since I like to include a set with each player I sell. Also keep extra HDMI cables, for the same reason. Once you reach that next level, it's nice to set up a testing station. Small TV, AV cables, and its ready for you to plug in. Video game systems- that's another great item to invest in as you grow. I will always pick up a Wii system if it's the right price. I don't pay more than $20 for a system with cables; more if it has games and accessories. I have a personal Wii for testing so if I pick up games, or guitars, I can be sure it works. This is true for other gaming systems as well, PlayStation, Xbox, etc. Having the systems to test is a bonus.

I always have an open mind to other categories as well: toys, cosmetics, pots and pans, golf clubs, sporting goods, hats, and so much more. These are all categories I am currently expanding in. Stay tuned in this book for how to get my free bonus list of BOLO's. BOLO is short for "Be On The Look Out".

CHAPTER 3
SHOULD I BUY IT?

This is the biggest question I get. This is always the biggest question in every reselling Facebook group. Someone is at a thrift storeand sends a picture of something. "Should I get it?" Well, the answer is, will it sell? Yes, I answered the question with a question, but that will always be the answer. You *must* look at comps. If you don't know what the item is, use a feature called Google Lens, downloadable as an app in the app stores, and snap a picture. It does a pretty good job of identifying something you may not recognize. You can then put that into eBay and comp it out. If you have to post to social media and wait for the group to reply, you are wasting time and missing out on other items in that store that someone else could be grabbing before you. If it's something that you don't know, and don't care to know about, then leave it. I have left many items on the shelves that I thought looked cool, but I couldn't find it online. Sure I could pick it up, run an auction, and hope for the best, but that's not my business model. I want to by stuff that sells, not sit on my shelf collecting dust.

The second part of this answer is how desirable is this item? Yeah you may like it, yeah it caught your eye, but how long will it take to sell? Unless you have endless storage, this should be a huge contributing factor to sourcing. You can easily figure out how fast something sells with comps. The sold listings on eBay go back 90 days. If you look up an item and it has 100 available and then you go to sold and there are 500 that sold in the last 90 days, you know it is a *HOT* item and you should grab it if the price is right. If an item has 100 available and only 50 sold, you know this item sells, just not as fast. I would still grab it. You want to make sure there is a decent sell through rate, or the amount sold vs what's available. I like to stay over 50% or close to it. Sure, there are exceptions if the price is right, but that's my general rule of thumb. Pricing really comes down to what you are comfortable with.

Starting out, I was fine making $20 on a $5 item. Today, however, I probably won't grab that item. Shipping, eBay fees, and time can make that an almost zero-profit item. Not so say this won't work for some, as it surely does. Just not for me.

Ok, back to this item. So you see it sells well, it's the right price, and now ask yourself, how easy is it to ship and store? If this is a larger item like a DVD player for example, I know I will need a special box. I know I need more packing materials, and I also need to take the time to test it. All those must factor into consideration if I want to make a decent amount of money on it. If there is only a $10, $20 profit I won't be picking it up. So, just ask yourself what your time is worth.

Researching your item is where the skill comes in. Anyone can say their item is worth thousands, but if it's not selling for that then it's not worth it. Simple. It is only worth what someone will pay for it. That goes for anything. That is why we see crazy items like a president shaped potato chip sell for thousands. Someone somewhere knew they had to have this chip, no matter the cost. This goes to show that anything and everything sells on eBay.

CHAPTER 4
PRICING

When you are searching for your items, and looking at what sold, take note of how much it is selling for. You will notice a decent range things sell for. Some have free shipping, some charge shipping, some auction, some sell using the "Buy It Now" feature. This will lead you to what should you price yours at. I like to price about 10-20% under the highest recent sold. I also use "Buy it Now" 99% of the time. Auctions are asking for trouble. They never sell for what you're hoping for. Yes, you can put a reserve, but that deters buyers and has an upcharge. So, I would rather price an item for what I want for it, and select "Allow Offers", giving buyers the option to submit offers for my item. I am never obligated to take an offer, but I firmly believe that leads to more sales. I will always consider their offer. If I feel it's fair, and I am still making good money, then I will accept. Usually, about 10% off is where I like. I will be more willing to negotiate when I have had that item for a longer time, just to move inventory. You can counter their offer if you feel it's not fair enough. After you submit a counter offer they have the option to counter back. The feature allows you to go back and forth up to 4 times. You can also turn on automatic decline on offers, under a certain amount, but I feel that closes a door on opportunity. If I think the offer is low, I just counter.

CHAPTER 5
FEES AND SUPPLIES

Every business has fees. Some at the front end, some on the back end. All businesses have a cost. eBay is no exception. You can cut cost when it comes to sourcing, and even getting some items for free, but you will have to pay when that item sells. The beauty of this is that your item *sold*! There is no worry about the fee, because you just sold your item; your fee comes right out of your profit. Too many people get dragged down complaining about eBay fees. I'm sorry, but simply just sell more stuff! Yes, they take about 13% of your sale. They also have listing fees if you have used up any free ones or promotional ones they have given. In my opinion, it is worth all of it! You get free traffic, and you get a platform to list on, that the entire world can see. You will *NEVER* find that for 13%! But this is a general number; that's what I average my fees are. Read up on eBay's latest fee schedule to find exact numbers if that excites you. My motto is "just sell more stuff". Having eBay manage payments now instead of PayPal has simplified that. No having to track fees and pay separately. It's all on eBay.

One way to cut back on fees is a store. This is something to consider as you grow your listings. Starter store for $5 per month gives you 250 listings and the Basic store for $22 per month gives 350 listings. You will also receive a coupon every quarter with the Basic tier worth $25 to be used toward eBay branded shipping supplies. Think *FREE TAPE*! However, you won't need to jump right into a store until you get more listings.

Speaking of tape, you will need a few supplies to get started in your eBay business. Some are essential, and others are great upgrades and worth it if you are taking this as serious as I think you are. First is a smartphone. This is how you will search items when you're out and about. Your phone can also be used as your camera for listings. You will also need internet access. Wi-Fi works fine, but you'll want something reliable. A printer is an item you will definitely want; and if you don't have one, worth grabbing even the cheapest one to start. eBay gives a shipping discount when you buy shipping on their platform. You can only take advantage of this by printing your label at home. You can print it out on basic paper and tape it to the box. Starting out I had some 2 per page adhesive labels I found online. I printed on an inkjet printer and stuck it to the package like a sticker. Next level and worth every penny is a thermal printer. I highly recommend the Rollo printer. This type of printer gets its hype because it never needs ink! It uses heat. The only supply it will ever need is 4x6 labels. This is an investment in your business and probably the best one yet. A scale is another. You can pick up a cheap scale online, on Amazon or eBay- just make sure it measures ounces. You cannot get an accurate weight for your listing, or for your shipping label, without it. Sure, you could go to the post office and have it weighed and then go back home to print, but that's a lot of effort. A scale is worth the $20 investment. The final item you will need, , is storage. You will want a space you can dedicate to inventory and supplies. Shelves are great, totes, boxes, whatever you want to use for your inventory system, but you need a place to put it. Preferably an organized space.

PRO TIP: Start an inventory system right away. Put item in said box, label box, and in your spreadsheet you're going to keep for bookkeeping, put that box number. This will save you so much time and energy when you go to ship. It may not seem like a lot when you have 3 items, but that will quickly become 200-300-400+ items and you'll wish you would have started at the beginning. I'm speaking from experience here.

Shipping supplies is something you can grow as you go. Have friends and family save all their boxes. We all are doing a little too much online shopping these days, so save those boxes and materials. You can get free priority mailing boxes from the USPS. You have to use those boxes only for shipping with USPS, but it's a great service. You can order directly from their website. You will also need tape, bubble wrap, packing paper— all things you want to be collecting. You can purchase this online, but get it free anywhere you can.

CHAPTER 6
SHIPPING

Cost

So, you've made your sales, and now you're ready to ship it! This tends to be the scariest part for some resellers starting out, but I feel if you learn the basics, there is nothing to be afraid of. eBay makes it pretty easy. Starting out, make sure you are charging "Calculated shipping". There is an option under shipping where you choose either flat rate, calculated, or free. Flat rate is if you just want to charge everyone $5, or something of the like, for shipping… NOT a safe game. Free shipping is great for traffic, but not great when you're starting out. That's a pro move after you get the hang of things. Stick to calculated as you are starting out. Be sure to enter the weight and size when you list. You can pre-box and weigh, or weigh it naked and add a pound or so for packing. Enter those into your listing to ensure you charge enough. Calculated shipping makes sure the rate is updated for them based on their location; this is the only way to ensure your shipping costs are covered. You can adjust the actual rate once it is boxed and you're about to print. Select the cheapest rate to ship as well as the correct cost. These shipping fees can be taken out of your pending balance or your checking account. You will select that under initial settings. Once you get more secure, you can offer free shipping on first class items. This will be $5-$7 to ship, and you can work that cost into your price. There is no such thing as free shipping—*ever* – someone pays for it, and in this case it's you.

Packing

Whether you weigh your item before or after packing it, you are going to need materials to ship it. There are a variety of options, from poly mailers, to nice-looking bags, to bubble mailers, and also boxes. Don't get intimidated. You want to pack your item well. Wrap it, bubble it, box it. Make sure it arrives at the destination safely. Use the smallest box possible, as size is money.

Poly bags will always be the cheapest, but not the safest, as there is no protection. You will enter the dimension of the bag before putting anything in it, for example 10x12x1. Use this for items that will not break in shipping. You can also get the best poly bag mailing rate using a service called *Pirate Ship*. Pirate Ship is a wonderful site. It is great for shipping anything, even outside of eBay. They use a cubic measurement rate that is the cheapest possible USPS discount to ship. If my item is heavy but small, always check the rates on Pirate Ship. Simply go to *pirateship.com* and make a free account. They even have the option for poly bags to make sure you get the best rates. Once you log in, you can link your eBay account, allowing you to "Import" those labels and print directly from Pirate Ship.

USPS has flat rate boxes; you will want to avoid a lot of those unless your item is super heavy. Rarely will those save you money. The only exception is the Flat Rate Padded Envelope. Those ship for $8, at the time of this publishing, to anywhere in the country. Small boxes are great. Anything under a pound can go First Class. Remember, don't use any USPS priority supplies for first class or you will be charged at a priority mail rate.

FedEx and UPS have negotiated discounts with eBay much like USPS. They are great for larger, heavier items. You will notice it's cheaper than USPS in those situations. I always look at them as an option when printing my labels.

"Global Shipping Program" is a service offered by eBay to ship your item overseas. While that may sound intimidating, if you are in the United States, you are only responsible for shipping that item to Kentucky. eBay then passes it on through customs and on its way. The only downside is, as a buyer, they have higher fees. I noticed to ship to Canada, for example, is awfully expensive with GSP, but I like it for the protection. You can always open up international shipping to Canada and charge the calculated rates directly. That can be saved for later.

The biggest thing with shipping is <u>practice</u>. Once you get the hang of it you could do it with your eyes closed. Get to know some free USPS boxes such as the shoebox, or the 1095 or 1092 for items like board games. These are great boxes that can fit items perfectly. Nice to always have on hand.

CHAPTER 7
YOU ARE NOW A
RESELLER

Congratulations on your first sale! I bet that fired you up as much as it did for me! Careful, its addicting.

The biggest take away I hope you learned is to buy it right in the first place. Do your research. Know what you're buying. Then there is no risk in taking an offer, in under charging shipping, in anything. You know you made a great buy and you're ready to sell. Buy LOW, sell HIGH. Buy anything low enough and you will make a profit. Enter this journey with an open mind. Learn new things. Know you will make mistakes as we all have when we first started. First and foremost, have FUN! I started this out as a hobby because I enjoyed it. It never feels like work to me. I hope you find that same passion, drive, and kick some eBay booty. Thank you so much for reading this far. I hope you learned a lot and are ready to put this into action. To eBay and BEYOND— ok, cheesy, but it sounded right. Happy Selling!

As an added BONUS and thank you for reading my book, please download a free copy of my PDF: My Top Selling Items That Sell On eBay at https://desertsellers.com/bolooffer

9 798709 492882